Sometimes the Blue Trees

Contents:

Sooner

than a puddle dries, the plane has boarded, I am calling
my grandmother, telling anybody who will listen

that I have a cheap radio I carry with me above my head,
and when you look at me you see a woman, but I'm pointing

without a finger at the radio I hold. I can stay on the couch
and not look at my radio, but only think I am so perfect

without anything-noise. I ask if you might like to listen,
but I cannot give you my hand to hold. If we are not alone

with ourselves long enough, it may be certain that everything
we ever held will kill us, or leave us alive in a green room,

with bright green lights and no air but lots of sound,
and many windows where nothing outside is green.

But the people can hear water and are making
themselves clean, and soon soon, the life is through,

but the people are not done, because they are asleep
and if I knew you, I might say Dear, Take a Rest Now.

But I do not know you so I will say. There. Be still.
Touch the place that hurts, and then go down

the street some more. Soon, I will find the last time
I climbed a maple tree, and we will walk home in shoes.

1

Finger painting

That's an example of something I can know
that's outside my experience.
Or else, you might start believing it, walking past,
and a few blocks ahead, more child-vacant sidewalk
art. Sight will tell you how to fix
no out-of-order bathroom.

I look at Stone Mountain growing its heads
of Confederate generals. I buy
a glow stick from the yelling vendor,
wave it as a private, children's flag.

There is mercury in the ice-cream here
I say after twelve bite-size bites. Something funny
about waiting in line for the summer night to descend
with family, or stories of it.

As we all know by now, power only has one chin,
because the angle we take its picture from is always up.

America is real crazy, for real.
My friend who is brilliant at hiphop
noticed that if she didn't have medication
she could be a crazy person on the train.

And, yeah, me too.

I am not in love with you
America, I just lost my way.
The primary colors are what they use
to instruct beginners on how to beg a canvas
to be its master. When I draw, I fake authority
by making bold and harsh lines.
Draw a portrait double
its normal size, and cast the background
of a thing in stark, harsh shadow.

Loneliness is an active verb

I have activated the minor lesson
that needs can be shopped for.
The uncertainty of entering
a super store with just a mind
and an empty rolling basket,
counting the days until
cubed cantaloupe goes bad,
or until the toothpaste aisle
goes on sale.

How come the father of my being
waits for no one, after I pull up
to the crib and yell "ready?"
He says, "I like the scissors
you use to tell a story
about who you are.
It's like you are a collage from bits
of paper, how you are stuck together
by kiddie glue, the eyes just bits
of wobbly black circle inside a white
circle, chasing themselves."

Friends of friends of friends
are carrying out their business
as usual, baking the usual
ovens for the usual lobster meats.
I am not in control, necessarily,
of what I have not begun
to believe in—
If I just want an ordinary
life, where might I cash in.

I say can I tell you a story:
there's a world in which everyone
is lonely, and there's one in which
everyone is not. I am
always anyone, and my eyes
sting from staying open underwater.
If I weren't everyone,

I could look out my window
at the Goddess of the Block,
and make her igloo
a paper sun to my door.

Another sad Black girl

enters the virgin planet
fist-first through a paint tube
arriving at a splattered palette
in the designated way.

My legs are cushions
against bats, hands of my bird-less dark
crossing over iridescent noise from
ass-loving howlers.

The virgin planet sings like this:
forgive, forgive, forgive, and believe.
But also: I be feelin' like things is fucked.

Even though I didn't resist the phone
when who's-his-name called, the play
ground has no closing hours when I put
on my chapstick and lather a sea-salt scrub
like wow.

Virgin Planet: No victims have yet donated
ears. But as we speak, the sad girls are
climbing steps, shrinking down their flower
poison into digestible xerox commuters.

Sad Black Girl: Be nice.

When I consider the African American

When I consider a broken arm that is now healed.
I remember that youth had its own ringtone,
its own set of physical gestures that will now be remembered
incorrectly. When I consider a broken leg I've never had.
I do not consider having wanted to be someone's wife,
more than wanting to meet a firm, unhidden silence while alive.
When I consider the broken fingers on separate hands.
I do not consider how a form of intimacy is drawn
when two people press their hands together.
I do not consider sticking my hand out the moving taxi
just so I could see the wind catch through my fingers.
See you in the drunk image of my mind, waiting at my door.
When I consider the broken septum, I do not consider
that it never actually did break, per se. Though my dad would say
it damaged the look of my face. The jewelry never really did much
but hang there, no skin ever broke through. When I consider
what I feel like when it's time to talk about Black people in history class.
My body is not left justified, my eyes are not center stage
seeking any type of white male professor to call me out
for a single line of verse, an insight. When I consider
the Negro Table at Atlanta Catholic High School,
I consider how my Black father told his son not to play
with that word. When I consider growing up being told
my family were the well-off ones of our family, I do not consider
that I am undeserving of the bracket of light I have claimed
outside the window trees. I am considering if I can be blameless
and still accountable. At breakfast my father dresses up his voice
in character, becomes Brutus Junior, the sweet man who serves
us our breakfast sausages. We would laugh and laugh
because we knew that it wasn't our father. When I consider
how the normal self-consciousness of a middle schooler rubbing
off her blue eyeshadow for fear of looking too made up
and still ugly, I consider how I still love that child.
When I consider what a stranger sees when they see me,
I do not consider it is possible that the site of brokenness
is no longer marked off with orange cones.

How to get over a millennial break up

I task myself with making home-grown mint
and walking the looped bicycle path
with a reusable bottle. I will not try on
a new shirt that I already have in a similar
shade of dark grey. When I was younger
I would count the number of friends I had
on my hands. Now, I count the number
of steps I have to take to burn off the guy
I kissed on a roof, after dancing badly
to a Starbucks playlist pop song.

I remember riding up an elevator
in the financial district wearing this very tight
black shirt—and I looked in the reflection
of myself in the silver sheen, and saw how
fat I was twenty pounds before this.
The emergency number to call for delusion
is not one I tend to save.

Instead, I stock up on rice cakes
and behave normally inside my own city
made up of no prize winners,
no naturally good swimmers, without
people who really do use tooth picks.
Actually, I would stare at my phone waiting
for a text from a boy I just decided I liked
because I saw him unwrap a fresh tattoo,
and we sat outside his house, him telling
me I was a bad kisser, even though
he did still visit me when I moved.
But the best part about ending it
is nothing ever has to be said
about the fact that I never took
any t-shirts, never collected any picture
frames, or names of relatives, only
saw them as a single action—the
way my lips sometimes feel when
they are allowed to be close enough
to feel.

To you / for you

I wanted for so long to write about what
a Black boy doesn't do before he kills himself.

If he doesn't sit in my therapy session
and tell me it's real dope to die. If he

doesn't write another song and ask
me if I get it, like if I get the part about

how a love ignites the gas within him.
If he doesn't run around the Grand Canyon

and then go back to my Southern grandma's
cabin in the Blue Ridge mountains, and release

some anger at how they originally rejected my dad.
If he is writing about summer in his journal,

and crosses a single line out that doesn't
fit. If his eyes are focused on the color blue

or if he can see anything at all.
If he knows that other Black boys will

die without their choosing it. If he will know
my parents will never say he chose it,

if it is okay to talk about this as a choice.
Why do I keep using that word. I keep trying

to write a poem. About this but the surface
won't let me go beyond a fact. I tell a fact

I tell a small detail. I try to think about sin,
where it lives in the face of a Black boy.

Why I bought a stupid bow and put it on my
head and wore it all the time. Because attention

never wears off. And the right kind, never gets old.
I want the attention of death. Look at me. Just look.

The need for power is crushing

And all the world is my trouble. Meanwhile, the observer is becoming
good at doing its task. At the principal beach the beach is an actor,
acting out Black ppl serving me/each other. The edges of society blur
like the side of a window overlooking the city lights/ Black on Black crimes.
Reality is a soft bellied woman. Tasks of a citizen include: slugging
a rope into knots and watching carefully its growth. An appeal

to the ground is not a dwelling place nor do I have the time.
Circle the viewfinder in all places it appears. I want for you, my lover,
to cross over that busy street, and run to me with food and no bricks
at all. Do not build me a single thing. Love is its own discipliner says a teacher.
Gripping at a relationship, I say. The sheer panic of not being able
to consume a rock sitting still in wet roots.

Language has no mission. English acquires more
and more knowledge. Words enter me as relationship.
This single brown bag I carry is my life. The structure of the sea
is new again as a boy rides his bike wiping the air
with his arms extended. The gap between his foot pressing down
and his realization of motion is slim and potent.

On a whim

I microwave Naan Pizza and Google
Image Blake Lively (the directions say
bake). Thinking about nothing in particular, I gather
my favorite selection of first names and say them aloud:
Ginger, Lallia, The American Girl Doll named Kit.
The names and I go out for a night of *girls get in for free.*
We wait our turn in line, before we end up on the toilet
peeing out boys we talk about between the awareness
of being sexual. Later, I am at home alone
thinking of myself as a drawer, and I put all the names
into my ear, stuff them directly into an unlabeled cabinet.
Other things belonging in the drawer, used gum wrappers,
a business card for eyebrow threading, loose dimes lying beside
threads of my hair. Sometimes, when I'm really nervous, I rehearse
in my head what I'll say in certain situations before I say it,
before even a question has arrived. I practice this now.
*No, I never have the urge to get in a car and drive on a windy road
and look at mountains. Yeah, I like my apartment, it's small but useable
space. Oh no, I'm not at all interested in being affiliated with
that, any of it.* Without thinking, I make the decision to look
at Blake Lively's hair. I do not think about how perfect it is
wet. I am in the middle of a passage in my book that talks
about being good, or less bad, to other people. It's a silly
thing to say in a book, when I'm thinking about being a
sexual person, and who I can text to see about my Naan
being cooled down enough to eat. I'm really very uninterested
in figuring out why I'm not thinking about what I care about
more. It's not that important if my mind makes a decision
before I can. Either way, one day I'm gonna trade this life
for the one I always thought someone else deserved.

For all the men I'll never write a poem about

My sadness has never lived unattached
as my happiness has. For example, say
a rapturous man appears on an average day.
Say I overthrow him, and we mate. I layer
a moment with my initials so that I can cover
the initials with more towels. I pile
the towels across a boring floor
so that nobody—especially me—will slip.
I remember, only after I am outside, to tell Rapture
there was an accident in the bathroom.
Afterwards, we cross our legs by the fireplace,
and say three things we like about each other.
I like that you are here, I like that I cannot identify you,
I like how you didn't notice that towels are covering up
the path to my house, I say eyes closed, mouth parted
for wisdom or want. The secret between me and Rapture
reminds us that we are never separate from our feelings
about each other. It is hard to say who is more real,
the feeling of having begun to yearn, or the movement
of taking away the towels and seeing the water has dried,
and I am still left over.

**Kanye praises colorism via casting call
or, Who got the Yeezy boost hookup**

The day Kanye graduated,
I got the CD, learned the verbs.
Kanye wears Kanye shoes,
elopes with Kanye in his backyard.
One of the first songs I loved was Kanye.
It took me back
to a day I hadn't lived yet,
made me lean out a window
and imagine I had a self
not too full to listen. A self-identified
self-annoys itself to death.
Is it Kanye of himself to appear now.
Little Kanye dangles his feet over the stoop
while his grandmother hums
a hymn she used to sing in the choir.
The best Yeezies are laceups, look
like snow boots, can be worn
in direct sun without discomfort.
Who am I to tell Yeezus dinner is ready,
but if he's hungry let him eat.
But if he's thirsty let him kill
a bear. Or a small panting fish,
an antelope with teeth.
Kanye is on babysitting duty
for the child I keep in a playpen.
Magic is our best pretend game.
Kanye is feeding a coral reef his gummy bears
his keep-it-clean-keep-it-cool blue silicone
mouthwash. To fall asleep, Kanye only sings
through the verse to one song
then runs it backwards once
with a fitted on his line up fresh.
Kanye holds the door open for you
until he gets really bored, and borrows
an old fur from his closet.
Kanye is a cut out paper doll
in a special collection series.
Kanye realizes Kanye's noodles

need to be boiling
before they can be eaten on a plate.
Otherwise, fill out the ABOUT ME section
and take off the plastic wrap.

An opaque center

I've never been the true Black
is a narrative that easily unfolds.
Define your terms.
True Black is a careful effort
of deterrence—my cousins unburnt
hands apply pressure to the leash
training the Rottweiler not to run away.
True Black wanted to descend as pre-bottled
erasure and family, but the borders between
the camping grounds and the permanent
address kept overflowing. True Black can be traced
diagonally to the name that matches the description
and back to the life that matches the name.
I wanted true Black to live inside my white
mother who homeschooled me and my brother,
taught me how to hold a pencil.
I wanted Black to be a universal,
a quality, a stipend for the lost map.
Ask: Whose map. Whose location.
I look at how long my mirror has
been at practice.
My true Black says look,
the folds and knots keep
rattling, the day keeps shattering
its rehearsals with new songs.

Black bachelorette

Is it more palatable
when a Black woman is proclaimed
beautiful an indiscriminate number of times,
when the indiscretion causes me to wonder
who is lying, and who is trying to cover the truth.

Is it more palatable
that the successful, beautiful and Black
woman chooses a white man over
a Black man. Is it more palatable
to a white audience to see their
fragile idea of Blackness confirmed.
The white audience inherits a Black woman—
She is the leg of a white man,
a legless stirrup, awaiting the foot
of a white man to take a ride.
A Black man helps steady her foot
into correct position. Lifts her heel
onto a television set. A white man
on tv sees her beauty, recognizes
what it might serve.
We love/Black people/on tv.

Is it so sweet how the interracial couple
is so in love and beautiful,
beautiful children they will make.
Light skinned and beautiful.
Good hair. So much love.

Do I love to see the white man
as taking the Black woman's ass in his
diamond-buying fist and fucking it raw
with softest kisses. Do I love the white man
more than myself.

The women and their shopping

I decided that instead of staying
indignant at my grossness, I'll lean
in. Maybe I'll be a consumption
queen. Let me count the ways
I have consumed today.
If I am being served time
by the Black man asking
me my order, if that is all
I want, will it trigger
the realization that not everything
which *feels* necessary needs acting on.
What if the 2 am morning tells
me I need a desperate donut.
And the 4 pm rainfall says I need
my lips to be a nice, audible plum.
There is no word for opening a gift
you already have. It's called belonging,
new bills to an old address, delivered on time.
Next, I rent my legs so I can use
them to run along the beach.

A strobe of neon occupies some room.
I want a new party hammock,
a new swan dove in silk. I want
seven ways to be alone with myself
without sitting in a room with walls.
I place my wants in plastic and take
them to-go. I buy my want not on discount,
it's the new thing I got in Miami on my day off.
I got my want so I can look good in it.
I ask my want who's driving, it tells
me not to ask any questions. I listen
while the music is turned up too loud,
and soon I am in the back seat having
my first slobber kiss with a boy I only like
because of his freckles. Sometimes,
want changes quick from hereditary to indigo.
What if my want is passed out on the dance floor
and the bar is no longer in service.

Can I tell the bouncer, *Look, I own that body.*
She just wants to go home. I don't have enough
for her ride, but if you could just let me stay
here with her. I just want to be alone. I just want
to know that if it's not enough, what is not enough
is not enough.

Immediate dangers

1. Can't wear my hat the same as *the others*.
2. Cut the top off my hat so they know I'm real.
3. Make an ode to various family members, seeking out the juicy parts of their story—jail, rape, etc.
4. I am made of biblical blood; I do not disappear in the dark.
5. The sermon about being humble before a male god.
6. In real time, the weather is medium, I got some food that's on the way (fried rice) and I'm lying on my round belly hearing night sounds.
7. My roommate did this thing once where she was like *perspective* and dropped the mic.
8. I picked the mic back up and entered the room.
9. You can't be Black in America and not have *perspective* as a side piece.
10. The tears I make are stolen from too long ago.

Am I crazy

When I arrived at the place for crazy people
I ordered green spinach and told the elliptical
I was gonna get it together, was gonna lose three to seven pounds
because if my mind was thin then my body would be happier.

I went to women's therapy and everyone had all the women problems
and I never spoke except sometimes I drew prismatic shapes
that looked like baskets holding tutus or tutus holding themselves
the pictures didn't have any meaning and that's what I liked best about them.

I sit on the lawn with a crazy guy who says he likes me, like we're in high school,
and I like him like I trust the grass with some of my words.
I am not ready to rise beyond painting therapy-headed pictures
of love and happy, of times when times when times when and happy.

One day I read a poem about being a passenger
that I wrote while I was in Malibu and full of depression and privilege.
It was mostly about death but all it talked about was trash and rats,
even though I don't think I'd ever been near a rat.

I took Adderall a lot, because that shit made my mind feel more active.
There was this very certain urgency to write something good,
so I would spend all night defining words in poems with the Oxford
Dictionary, but taken apart to mean something else.

Before I left the place where I was supposed to become sane
I talked to this lady about my brother and how I couldn't talk about myself
without talking about him and she said that's the first time she felt like
she ever got to hear from me.

The tailors say unfastening builds a more likable present, the way your dog is
both charming and yours. The clear glass needs mini mountains of sparkle in
order to breathe out, simply utter a rejection. What kind of presence dilates
without engulfing a green lawn in soaps.
They can see you breathing. Don't look away.

National anthem

The pain of others
gently stabs me like
the slow entrance
into a scalding tub.

As we place the bright flowers
at my brother's grave,
I think to make folded birds
across a sea of black openness.

The door I enter through
welcomes wanderers of all kind.
The strangest bird can still fit
through the door even when
it is walking slow or fast— even
if it only remembers that once it was a bird,
with no hands, and a memory
of where a tree in the world is not blind.

Rihanna would be more beautiful white

The symmetry of Blackness is just off, like in order to see it you gotta twitch or convulse, you can't just be sitting still staring blankly at the dog, waiting for something to miracle away from Black, so when the horse is dismounted and the sun been turned off, it's not that something emerges from a void, but that whatever was already seeing stops to miracle color.

Writing about Blackness is profitable for the Black woman knows it's profitable and uses it. So that Blackness becomes its own scheme in the making of a new, fresh white. As if wearing a #BlackLivesMatter tee makes her skin more black, makes her think more Blackly—in terms of being always aware of what one is not.

The selfishness of being Black is to not allow anything else in. A full load is carried out each day, left to wake up in the air. When we next wake up, we take care to love who is not there.

Black history month

My father bends below the Christmas tree
making sure it's watered.
He has been awake for so long.

He started working at Waffle House
in management when my brother was born
because he needed a real job.
When I was born he had to work holidays.

Business gets him up at five
when he'll go for the morning run.
He drinks his coffee black without sugars or creams.

My dad likes to keep things scary neat,
is a regular flosser, does not approve
of my disregard for manicures.

On a hike once, he tried to teach
me how to casually smile
at strangers. The simple dirt beneath us.

On a Christmas morning, he sits
on the couch beside me. In space,
but seeing the spaces in time, almost
physical.

You have to feel these things too, I say.
He had to identify
my brother's body. He knows how mangled
limbs appear in the face of his son.

I am happy that my father only captures
the chipmunks in our yard when he is home,
so they can soon be set free elsewhere.

His favorite salad is the one with walnuts up the street.
That custom-made suit in blue is his. And when
he played college basketball he was still very tall.

Elijah

My brother's room was painted
pale green. He was not
a poet, but he went to Barnes and Noble
and recited "Two roads diverge"
to various unasked audience members.
He really loved Kanye,
especially the *Graduation* album.
For his first album, he wanted
to write about Atlanta Catholic High School.
I went with him back to our
school and he had this recorder,
and he went through the halls opening
and shutting lockers and tapping on things,
taking their sounds from them.
When he was eighteen,
he moved to New York and he took
my mom's split pea soup recipe with him.
When we were at his apartment with
his best friend, cleaning
up his things after he died, picking up his stacks
of composition notebooks, his sweatshirt
he wore when he met Questlove. My mom
kept repeating that all the ingredients
for split pea soup were laid out in the small
kitchen, like he was about to make it.

When he was younger, he wrote this song
that said, "got me feeling like Elijah the world
out to get me, but I aint scared of it, I aint
scared of shit." A part of the chorus is a sort
of anthem to suicide, and when I wanted
to feel really joyous, I would listen to it after
he was gone. I don't know where the song is
now. Davis had this vocal coach who worked
with Justin Bieber, and before he died he was
in the process of writing a song for Beibs.
I found out my freshmen year of college
that he'd started taking anxiety medication,
I never knew anything was wrong before that.

At the time, I thought being on medication was
very serious, and something was very wrong
with him. Which is funny now. One time, right
after we moved to California, I got mad at him
for some reason and put all his stuff in the
bathtub. If you don't know what mental health issues
look like, you don't know when they are present. I see that now.

At a steakhouse we ate at a lot as a family,
Davis was talking about his new girlfriend,
whom he'd met at a party, how she was very
independent and smart. I remember worrying
that I was neither of those things and that's
why men didn't want me. Before he went to college
Davis wrote me a handwritten note saying I was
one of his best friends. He also wrote one for his
ex-girlfriend. She posted it on social
media after he died. She's pretty, I follow her on social media.
When I moved to New York I wanted to do what
Davis did in the school halls, I thought I could
walk around the city and somehow record his
sounds. Driving to a family member's house
in Florida, Davis was telling us how this producer
in Atlanta said the word "phenomenal" really funny-
like fo-nom-en-ah. And we thought it was very
funny, and we were just laughing and laughing.

Poem for my mother

If a mother is hurting
no thing can stop her.
A paper maché family tree
mantels her movements,
makes it so all the real
trees only look like the paper
hanging down her eyes.

Except sometimes the blue trees
do not refuse her sight. They look
and look and see her.
I keep a collection
of mothers on my mantel.
Some are life-size while others
can't surely fit in the room.

I once asked how they got there.
We have no home, they chanted.
They have expanded with time
like the dolls you place in water.
To fuel a mother,
turn off the lights, press
the small of the neck against the breast

and project images of her childhood.
Tell her she can own any
one of these images, it can be hers.
Because time is heavy
and air is less thick
than the blood on your hand,
pricked by an angry weed.

Mother, I can't go any deeper into blood.
As soon as I say sorrow,
it disappears.
And I mean it that Jesus will be back soon
and he will care for you.
Even if we cannot be
disciples of the dead.

Poems do not die

After a room goes stale
with the heat of loss,
            it must be exited.

Only after it is left, can you re-enter.
Only then, does the room die.

            When I walk in
to the dead room, I see how human
it is to be alone.
            It is just me with the dead
thinking about entering a room
                  and exiting it, without being seen
thinking about hallways, so many hallways
            all pale green and soundless.

There are rooms for the dead
Inside of me.   I keep
them very clean. Do not touch
the walls or the room will die.

            I look at my brother's
face, I look at it so long I almost forget
            I'm in the hallway.
Why did he leave
his dead room behind.

Ode to the only Black woman reading a poem

I believe that in her first iteration, the Black woman
                was complete sentences.
I believe she is clothed in righteousness
                with a fresh glaze of Eco-Styler.
I believe in the Black woman
                as a filing cabinet for what will be used later.
I believe that her last breath moves
                toward another since it's never just the one
woman tying a boot, kissing a blanket,
                making a hotel for the burden to lie or sleep.

I believe that a journey is undone
                when a Black woman calls down
from her place of purpose and says,
                I have finished my work in the home.
I believe that a recipe can cook more
                than its original dosage.
I believe that in making the full pan,
                a Black woman has chosen to breed an abundance
that is new for each day.

If I believe in the Black woman,
                I too must believe in her frame:
that she is both bound by the ideas of herself
                and in love with them. Her hair, her clothes,
her speech, she loves them, as you do.
                But she will not show
you how she is undone: taking off her lipstick,
                saying a shallow prayer against hate.

Flat tummy tea
or, Do you want me because I am lost

I am cross-eyed and peeping
beautiful girls' Instagrams.

I sit across from my mouthed therapist,
and she's saying shit like, your family

never fucked with emotion. I want to tell
her the master of emotion is a white

pawn. I don't know what kind of black
my grandfather is, and I'll never grieve

the lives I do not know. Just yesterday,
I was realized without my history,

as a brown girl from California who talks white.
Born and bred on those white lands

of beaches and beaches with voices
that chirp without pain or honey.

Can I live
or, the Black man as god

I want the good pussy,
which is to say— the pussy
with the marble floors, all tile
actually, a surround sound pussy.
I want to gargle, and to spit
back up the original sin
of the pussy doing its thing,
all by its independent pussy self.
Like how many ways can I love
a pussy before it breaks. If she
can talk that's a plus but that ass
gotta be ready to stop, drop, and roll,
cuz lemme tell you I been thinkin'
bout that pussy so much, want a pic
of that pussy to show my boys.
Even if you tell me not to look
I'll look at you like I already
owned that pussy long before
it was alive. You see the thing
is I love that pussy. That's mine.
Like how you can love a thing
so much you gotta break it
so you can love it even more.
That's how. Watch me while
I remove your shirt, watch
me while I make your tongue
my tongue, while I invert
our positions into what I like
to see, how I like it when your
pussy walks down the street
thinking of me, like how we
can never hold hands in the street
cause that shit look too pregnant
with live bacterias. It gotta be
way cooler than that. Like we
been soaked each other in cool
whip and now it's time for the pitbull
fight. But seriously, call me later

girl, after I make this money
I want that pussy to sit on top
my bills, lick `em real good,
till they cleaner than a naked
chicken, already baked and headless.

I hate home so much that I build it every time I sleep

As an ordinary citizen of the world
the absence of an ideal does not become me.
Who she is without boundaries,

no views no views no views to bind
to a purely innocent throat. I have wanted
to look at my childhood self and say she is finished.

Looking in the mirror, at my mind,
the way a man acknowledges he has a beard.
If I am running around a big tree

and the failed relationships are standing
around me as tall trees, as full-grown men.
If the men counsel people on how to finish

growing a tree. He counseled me on how to race.
And then I looked down, looked at my hands
shut my eyes, and he became me.

And then my hands were bulletproof
and bloody. In the home I grew
up in the stucco was not new

the trees were green the trees were green.
I am running like a female deer moving inside
a human house, soundless and full of rage.

Daddy issues
For Philando Castile's daughter

Dear daughter of a dead black man,
Did you re-learn the ABCs from your dead words.
Did you want all those strangers gifting you prayers.
Did the light beside the casket choke you
back to the school yard, jumping rope in free air
with three friends you call by other names
because it's fun. Did you press the inside of your
ear when you heard the sirens, to make it seem
like your ear had made it happen, and your ear
could stop it whenever it just wanted to not
be Black. And did you listen to the people who told
you to make peace with the ones who did it, did you
learn that the tools for forgiveness do not come
free of charge to the Black woman, to the Black daughter,
to the little Black girl without a father. Did you learn
that you too are Black, and did you learn to be afraid.
Did you learn to chase fear, and to choose it.

Let me let you come in

When I've been driving a green-stopped road
and blasting the persona of fragile cinnamon,

I smell you, as a courage to direct scent
into a world you belong inside. With dogs or trees
or something as un-beautiful as being part
of a place that is not beautiful.

I realize my spirit-guide has missed their train stop miles back
but I learned not to call them doesn't rarify the wellspring.

What I know of the never-ending love of paper bags is that
if you give me time, I'll stop holding one over your face.

Ten days to self-esteem

Outside an Atlanta hookah bar
I wear a Compton beanie, and laugh
a white laugh at how it's funny to not
be from Compton. Some days, I'll tell
you I grew up across from
the *Father of the Bride* house. I am used to fancy
juice shops, and ordering what I'd like.

It's funny to talk about race when you're
outside it. Given that I check yes
to any question involving *Oh you don't look Black tho*.
Given that anyone can tell a bumper sticker
from the film of glue it might leave if removed.

In my best life, I am something of a vegan spiritual queen,
living out the soul of drum beats. I tithe with raw mango,
see the shadow of myself as the whole love of a planted tree.

The role of a poet is to represent some truth.
When I forget the truth, I might refer to any number
of dangling bodies I've encountered to my left or right
in moments not meant for my taking.

I ring the doorbell of my grandfather's house
where he calls back from the war,
telling of my grandmother's butter skin.
He puts on a shirt that's technically brown
and tells me marriage is on the horizon.

I ring the doorbell and my grandmother spells out
the eating of her plants by deer.
We chat about what it's like to work in a jail,
if tasers are used, how frequently.
I think the rolls might be better served
with a more elegant napkin, maybe a monogrammed lace.

I am on a family couch.
I rake myself into useable form.
The leaves are sizable and red.

Look, a family from the South
playing outside with their kids.

Sometimes, nothing deserves praise.

On limits

No man can guard me
from myself when I look
in the mirror, and see
both the sun in the maple
and the body of a woman
yelling through the tall grass
to get off her property
before she calls the police.
In a little while I will be hungry
to mix my hands with dirt,
and praise the fallen ground.
I am not yet a woman.
I am not yet a woman.
I am not yet a woman.
What sun has not yet come
I do not miss.

The most natural

Naturally, in the deservedly spoiled hours of the night I am un-lonely. I un-see all the excellence of my own doing. Tripping over a stray piece of trash, I re-download Tinder, and marvel at all my makeup with missing tops.

If I want to return to the natural, I un-mystify my need to be placed at some beginning point. I un-remember my divine aspiration to be a basketball wife. I un-place the band aid on my three-year-old toes. Most things that have not been left off while waiting for something natural, like fear, to occur.

I un-watch the home videos where the snow is natural and the red coat is natural and love is natural. I am unstuck out of my apartment, I am un-calling my roommates, unthinking of places to go. Now, it is yesterday again. Where it is natural that the Sangria fruits are stewing. Or if I can't find an end, I might receive no joy from being right here.

A beautiful poem

If nothing confines
a man like strength
then nothing confines
a woman like beauty.
And if a woman is beauty
she must know how
beauty moves, must
study beauty only,
how it may possess
her, take over her sleeves,
direct the thumbs
into the pockets, take out
a ticket made for the entrance,
takes her into a dance hall
where beauty is courting
her. Tracing her around
the floor. Minding her
steps so that nobody
takes her hands except
the beauty that fills
the room, or if she breathes,
it is that pause which might
cancel out her illness.

Though I have forgotten
before to mention she was
ill, it is true, she is both
beautiful and ill and it
is not certain yet which
is more. Though beauty
does not take a liking
to being less than any
other thing. And I might
as well say it—I am rather
obsessed with the idea
that I am the only
thing in the room as soon
as I take to putting on
my beauty, truly it is

finished. And if you
don't mind, would you
please just give me a moment,
I must re-apply the lessons
I have learned from love.

Fratricide

I am supposed to be
asleep in the shower
vomiting up the kiss
from years ago,
your front lawn,
our fruitless sabbath.

I stalk the lemons at the store,
tell each one I am blessed.

I haven't felt pleasure in years
least of all
from a small creature
of the earth.

Yesterday, in a dimly lit room
I do not remember
old loves, do not love,
each time I say suicide,
each time I'm alive.

Girls just wanna have emotions they can see on rings

Whereas, being flawed, I always try
to write the poem I cannot write.
I enter into my mind like a camper
too hot or too cold in my tent. Ask
it questions like *how many times*
do you need to pee before you will
be hungry again, tell it things like
certain dumb bitches (me) *can still be average*
in certain spaces. A small hollow
is a metaphor for hands is a metaphor
for when I'm not crazy. I'm just desperate
for truth to be more risen in light than it is—
for light to be other than liquid yellow
or a way to surrender my ability to know
which way home is when I'm outside
near a train at night.

I am not saying ya'll ain't never been mad like me.
But, I am saying, *Try me.* Why you gotta
tell me, *you act white,* but then put on your
nigga lips and call me *gurl* eight times.
Like who actin out. I guess I just feel like
the problem is I got some, and I keep
naming them, and then as soon
as I think I got them all named and gathered,
one runs away, and I gotta start all over
again.

For example, I want to know
why brother is a word used
for anyone you love, and why everyone
but my brother deserves
hurt—

When I arrived on your back
I was toothless but wanted to bite
into something too large to see.
To see if the blood might make me kneel
after all. I am walking around drunk now,

feeling like the party didn't come to me.
Or else, I am skinning my knees for the chance
at being redeemed through punishment.

If I am raw in the worst way then nothing
can come through but peace,
I will say to myself in the dark.
I will say to myself in the dark that I don't love
anything, because I knew after being told
I had privilege, after being told I was white,
after learning that Black girls don't part
their hair down the middle like I did,
I learned to keep thinking about a way to resolve
the middle part. I haven't come up with an answer
that doesn't need time to take another walk.
What if I'm not waiting, what if I already know
I can't ever stop being Black, now what.

Pacific Coast Highway

When I am at the gas pump in LA and I'm not thinking about blue jeans, I resurrect the idea that something simple can be nice: a friend who has more than one name for me, being alone when alone is not a state of mind— practically speaking, being heard in the small auditorium of my mind, and having the auditorium empty out single file, while noticing the air in the room, noticing how my body feels a part of itself.

I need to write a poem about symbolic roots, or if it ever happens that in my more beautiful days the un-symbolic light could whisper to me. I can remember being small, the stillness. The air.

When I was small, I got housed by the perception of congruity. The path down to the river was narrow, but we would never come back home without a story to tell. The mud itself was a story. Later, we called back to a summer, asking it why the part of the bed we jumped on never talked back. When we grew up, it happened that the tie-dye card with birthday plans on it kept receiving cold guests who had checked out from the party years back. Paper dolls, paper maché, paper lanterns, papery trees. The difference is we know the thing when we touch it.